The Overthinking in Relationships Fix

Toxic Thoughts That Can Destroy Your Relationship And How To Fix Them

By

Rodney Noble

Table of Contents

Introduction

If you are or have been in a relationship, one thing would be clear to you: they almost always lead to an overthinking mind. A simple, unanswered text may lead you to obsessively refreshing your social media. You keep thinking if their boss is making them work late or if they are willingly ignoring you. Similarly, an off-hand comment regarding their partner ex may spark a Sherlock Holmes in you, ready to spark an investigation about how "over" they are about their last relationship.

The problem with this irritating yet completely normal pattern? Overthinking.

Despite knowing that it's not going to get you anywhere, you continue to do it over and over again. With so much overthinking and the anxiety that often accompanies it, you do not remain in touch with your intuition. This loss of connection with your intuition makes you less cognizant of what's going on in your relationship. Moreover, it can also take out the real fun of the relationship, too.

Just think about it.

How many times in the past, did you hear your partner say, "stop overthinking it?" You may have dodged this question with an answer like, "I don't think that you are thinking it through enough," or "I am not sure what you mean. "A lot of times, it is the communication that's behind all the misunderstandings you face in a relationship. You say one thing, but your partner understands it differently. This complication becomes worse when you acquire the awful habit of overthinking, which is simply a way of processing information a lot more than it is necessary.

When you are overthinking, you are pulling from a much bigger pool of information than necessary to accomplish your task. This fact holds true no matter what problem you are facing - be it you thinking of why your partner comes home late after work or wondering if your partner still finds you attractive.

Every single person who's ever been in a relationship is guilty of overthinking at some point, which makes the relationship much harder than it should be. All the negative thoughts keep swirling around in your brain, turning the tiniest inconveniences into full-blown arguments with your partner later.

What's more, overthinking can make you acquire an emotionally damaging mindset. A mindset in which you start thinking negatively not only about yourself but also about your partner and the world in general. With too much negativity all around you, you will be incapable of spotting any hope of positive thinking or finding a path to becoming a positive person regarding your relationship.

Is that what you want? Certainly not.

So, if you consider yourself an overthinker who is on the verge of breaking their relationship, this book is your only hope of survival. It will take you on a journey where you will discover many things about yourself as a person.

Many people spend their entire relationship living with all the chaos going inside their mind and fail to reach out for help. As a result, their relationship dies before it can fully blossom. But you are not going to be one of those people. Not in this life. The simple fact that you have consulted this book for help is your first step forward.

With this book, you are going to shed your old, chaotic mindset and find clarity. You are going to find a way through all the noise inside your mind that turns you against your partner all the time. You are going to war against your brain to save your relationship, and with this book, you are going to come back as a survivor.

So, if you are ready, let's begin.

Overthinking And Its Effects On Your Relationship

It is unarguable that overthinking is destructive for any relationship. This fact does not only apply to your romantic relationship with your spouse. Overthinking can equally damage your connection with your friends, colleagues, kids, parents, and everyone that has come in contact with you even once.

But how does overthinking destroy relationships? Where does it source its destructive abilities? The answers to this question form the content of this chapter.

Relationship Anxiety

Consider that you are in a relationship with the most amazing person you have ever met. You love and trust them, and over time, you have even learned the conversation styles of each other. Yet, your mind sometimes makes you doubt it all: you, your partner, and the bond between them. Numerous thoughts keep crossing your mind all the time.

- "Will this relationship last?"
- "Is this person the right one for me?"
- "Are they hiding any secrets from me?"
- "Am I even capable of maintaining a healthy relationship?"

Thoughts like these continue to wander inside your mind as you struggle to keep your relationship from breaking apart. Confused, you try to figure out what's causing these thoughts. Lucky for you, there is a name for this type of constant worrying: relationship anxiety.

Relationship anxiety refers to the feelings of insecurity, doubt, and worry that may pop up in the minds of two committed people. This type of anxiety does not necessarily indicate a failed relationship. It may even hit you if everything is going well with your partner.

Five Signs Of Relationship Anxiety

Relationship anxiety can take up many different forms and give rise to various manifestations. The following are some potential signs that may indicate underlying relationship anxiety.

Wondering If You Are Important To Your Partner

As a sufferer of relationship anxiety, you may worry if your partner deems you important. For example, you may worry that:

- Your partner won't miss you if you are not around them.

- Your partner may not offer any support or help if you encounter anything serious.

- Your partner is simply with you because of what

you do for them.

- Stressing that they want to break up.

Every good relationship makes you feel secure, happy, and loved. So, it is perfectly normal to feel every now and then the fear of losing what you have at the moment.

However, when these thoughts take the form of a persistent fear that your partner might leave you, things get dangerous. This constant anxiety becomes more problematic when you try adjusting your behavior to secure your relationship.

For example, you may:

- Avoid highlighting issues that hold importance for you, like frequent lateness.

- Ignore things your partner does that bother you, like wearing dirty shoes inside the house.

- Stress a lot about the risk of your partner getting

mad at you, even when they do not seem angry at all.

Doubting Long-Term Compatibility

Relationship anxiety may raise questions regarding the compatibility between you and your partner. These questions may arise; even your relationship is going great. Things get worse when you start questioning if you are happy in your relationship or if you just think you are. As a consequence, you start focusing your attention on all the minor differences between you and your partner. For example, you may notice how your taste of music differs. Then, you overemphasize the importance of these differences, which ultimately creates blocks.

Sabotaging The Relationship

Sabotaging behaviors often have a deep link with relationship anxiety.[1] To connect the two factors, you first need to understand the signs of sabotage which include:

- Picking up arguments with your partner more frequently;

- Pushing your partner away by insisting that nothing's wrong when, in fact, you are in clear distress;

- Testing the boundaries of your relationship, for example, grabbing a bite with your ex without letting your partner know.

You might not be doing these things on purpose. However, the underlying goal of these actions is almost always to find out how much your partner truly cares.

Reading Into Their Words And Actions

If you tend to keep thinking about what your partner said or did, you might be suffering from relationship anxiety. You may constantly think about why they don't like holding hands. Or why do they insist on keeping their old furniture when you move in together.

Sure, these signs may indicate a potential issue in some cases, but in many others, it is just because they have sweaty hands or love their old sofa set.

Causes Of Anxiety In Relationships

Relationship anxiety can have several reasons: some of them are serious, while others are not. Nevertheless, relationship anxiety is a constant struggle. It is something that you want to get rid of as soon as you get a diagnosis.

The following are some common causes that may trigger relationship anxiety.

Loss Of Trust In The Relationship's Future

Trust is an extremely important part of a relationship.

It is the trust that forms the very basis of every relationship. Once shattered, it is very difficult to rebuild. The biggest and the most common cause of anxiety in a relationship is the uncertainty about its future. This uncertainty may arise from frequent fights, growing distance, or previous history of breakups. Irrespective of the cause, when a relationship loses its trust, the uncertainty it leaves behind generates anxiety.

Walking On Eggshells

Frequent fighting in any relationship can be problematic. The main problem behind frequent fighting is not only the fact that it involves anger, but it also includes the feelings of worry that you will fight again.

This worry can generate relationship anxiety since you get too afraid to do anything in the presence of your partner.

Negativity

Negativity is a part of most struggling relationships. This negativity is what hinders you from acting friendly and supportive of each other. All your playful jokes become negative, and you often use your words in an argumentative tone and for criticism. This constant flow of negativity from all sides appear to exacerbate anxiety in relationships.

Stress

Stress is perhaps the most important reason behind relationship anxiety. It is more common in struggling relationships as compared to the stable ones. This stress tends to develop over time and may even pave the way for anxiety disorders. The reason behind this stress can be anything. Maybe both of you are struggling with finances, careers, or sexual life.

When you are in a stressful relationship, you feel stressed all the time. Eventually, this converts into anxiety and makes the situation worse.

Self-Build Problems

Another way how overthinking can negatively affect your relationship is by creating problems when they are non-existent.

Consider this scenario:

You are sitting idle on your couch when suddenly your mind starts wondering where your partner is. They told you they'd be working late, but are they? What if they just made an excuse to avoid you and hang out with their ex? Even though they just called you from their office phone, maybe they have called over their ex in their office so that you don't get suspicious.

Eventually, you feel that it is impossible to get rid of these feelings. Instead, these thoughts start dominating you. You are unable to break out of it, no matter how hard you try. Although you realize how your concern is extremely irrational, it does not stop you from worrying about it. Helpless, you may tend to seek reassurance from other people yet, the worry keeps on returning.

What happens eventually is that you get caught in a worry cycle. This state is extremely frustrating, paralyzing, and overwhelming experience for many. In these circumstances, the worry seems untriggered and so random that you are always anxious about almost everything.

Unable To Enjoy The Time You Actually Spend With People

Overthinking can most definitely create a storm of thoughts inside your head. It does not matter the place you are or whatever you are doing; there is a thinking cycle continuously going on in your subconscious mind. This phenomenon hinders you from actually enjoying time with the people around you since your mind is always on some other problem.

For example, if you constantly overthink how your partner might be cheating on you, it would become impossible to get rid of this thought. Even if you are out with your friends to grab dinner or away with your best friends for a vacation, your mind will always be thinking about what your partner would be doing at the same time.

In short, overthinking will hinder you from enjoying the present while worrying about what could happen in the future.

Overthinking: It May Affect A Lot More Than Just Relationships

By now, you must be clear about how overthinking can affect your relationship with your partner as well as other people around you. However, the effects do not stop here. Obsessively thinking over issues related to your relationship can also take a toll on your physical and mental health.

Impact On Your Health

Anxiety constitutes a normal part of life. For instance, you may feel it right before going for a job interview. This anxiety may increase your heart rate and breathing, improve the blood flow to the brain, and much more. All this physical response occurs to prepare you to face the situation that follows. However, if you keep spending most of your time overthinking and feeling anxious, you may start feeling its detrimental effects on health. Constantly overthinking and making yourself anxious all the time can exert devastating effects on both your physical and mental health. To make it worse, some of these effects are even irreversible.

Physical Effects

The following are the physical effects that you can encounter due to overthinking and consequent anxiety.

Central Nervous System

Overthinking for extended periods can lead to long-term anxiety and panic attacks. These attacks trigger the release of stress hormones daily, which causes symptoms like dizziness, depression, and headaches.[2]

When you feel stressed or anxious, the brain floods your body with chemicals and hormones designed to deal with stress. Cortisol and adrenaline are examples of such hormones. While these hormones are extremely helpful in coping with stressful events, their long-term exposure can harm your physical health. For example, a high level of cortisol in your blood for long durations of time can cause weight gain.

Cardiovascular System

Too much-overthinking leads to anxiety, and anxiety can cause an increase in heart rate, chest pain, and palpitations. It can also increase the risk of several cardiovascular disorders, including hypertension. If you are already a heart patient, overthinking can increase the risk of further complications and active coronary events.

Digestive And Excretory System

Overthinking and anxiety can greatly affect your digestive and excretory systems. You may suffer from nausea, diarrhea, stomach aches, and other digestive problems. Sometimes, loss of appetite may also occur.[3] Studies have suggested a connection between anxiety and irritable bowel syndrome. IBS is an autoimmune disease that includes bouts of diarrhea alternating with constipation and can be discomforting.

Immune System

Overthinking and the anxiety it causes may trigger the fight or flight response. In turn, the body releases several chemicals like adrenaline in the system. In the short term, it may increase your breathing rate and pulse so that your brain gets more oxygen. Moreover, your immunity may also get a boost. All this occurs to prepare you for the upcoming stressful event. However, if you keep feeling anxious due to repeated overthinking, your body continues to stay in this state and can never return to normal. This weakens your immune system and makes you vulnerable to infections of all kinds.

Respiratory System

Overthinking stresses you out and may often cause you to experience rapid, shallow breathing. If you are already a patient of any respiratory illness, like chronic obstructive pulmonary disease or increased anxiety levels, may land you in the hospital. Furthermore, increased anxiety can also worsen the symptoms of asthma.

Other Effects

Other effects that may occur due to overthinking include:

- Headaches;

- Muscle tension;

- Frequent sleep disruption;

- Social isolation;

- Insomnia;

- Low energy levels;

In addition to the physical effects described above, overthinking and its consequent anxiety may also cause mental distress.

The Risk Of Mental Illness

Do you feel like you always fixate on your past mistakes? Dwelling on your problems, mistakes, and shortcomings of the past may increase your risk of encountering mental health problems. Overthinking sets you up for a vicious cycle that is extremely hard to break. It may wreak havoc on your life and your mental peace and introduces you to various mental diseases.

Problem-Solving Ability

As an overthinker, you are likely to overanalyze things. You believe that rehashing certain situations or problems in your head can help you overcome them. However, studies have proven otherwise. According to experts, overthinking can reduce your ability to solve problems. This reduction occurs because you stick with the same problem and start imagining situations that may never occur instead of looking for a solution.

When the problem exacerbates, making simple choices like choosing what to eat or wear can become life or death situations.

Self-Esteem

People who struggle with problems like overthinking and resultant anxiety commonly struggle with the issues of low self-esteem. They often have low confidence and consider themselves as worthless. Low-esteem can be an extremely harmful symptom that indicates that the sufferer is on their way to develop a generalized anxiety disorder.

The Self-Esteem Theory

The self-esteem theory asserts that humans have evolved to experience social avoidance and inclusion emotionally. Experts believe that the level of self-esteem relies on how much rejection or acceptance you face in the social world. You develop self-esteem because you view how people react to you. So, automatically, you will have high self-esteem if you get a lot of acceptance from people, and a low one if you face more rejection.

The problem that most people experience is that they fail to read the level of acceptance and rejection they receive from other people. This failure causes people to have low self-esteem when, in fact, they are getting a lot of acceptance. This phenomenon commonly occurs in those who have anxiety secondary to overthinking.

Having low self-esteem can significantly affect personal relationships.[4] It can give rise to imbalances, insecurity, and arguments and may let you face the g problems:

Your Needs

If you have low self-esteem, it may become difficult for you to ask your partner or anyone else for help. You may get this feeling that you are increasing their mental burden or are a source of inconvenience. When you start masking your needs, you will automatically start getting the feeling that your partner does not care for you, which will further distance you from them.

Sensitivity

If you have low self-esteem, you may take simple requests from your partner personally. For example, if your partner wishes for some quiet time, you may get hurt and feel rejected. These feelings of rejection may cause you to recoil or snap back at your partner to start an argument.

Jealousy And Insecurity

Low self-esteem can also lead to insecurity and jealousy in a relationship. You may start questioning your worthiness to your partner and feel like you are unimportant. You may also feel like your partner is more attached to someone else or fear that they may leave you.

Difficulty Being Yourself

Low self-esteem can make it hard for you to be your true self in your relationship. You may feel that you are putting a considerable effort into being attractive or likable. For example, you may have to work hard to feel attractive for your partner.

Patterns Of Overthinking And Their Fix

Overthinking in relationships can be of different types. Some people waste time ruminating about their past while others worry about the future. Each of these types has its consequences and can disturb your relationship and life in many ways.

Ruminating About The Past

Consider the following scenario:

You are at work and the days seem to be going pretty great. You are looking forward to spending a relaxing evening at home. Fifteen minutes before you leave your workplace, your boss shows up and informs you how you have messed up a project. You try apologizing and explain what it occurred; however, the boss decides not to listen and keeps confronting you.

Situations like these are quite common in daily life, and almost everyone faces them at some point. In most cases, such situations leave you in a pretty bad mood too.

To deal with such a situation, you have two options:

1. Go home and enjoy your evening as you had already planned, leaving your work problems in your office.

2. Carry this problem back home and keep thinking about how your boss treated you unfairly today.

In most cases, you will choose to go with the second option. You will keep replaying the problem over and over in your head. This process that you will be engaging yourself into is rumination.

Rumination refers to repetitively thinking about the cause, situational factor, and the result of an emotional experience, which is mostly negative.[5] In simpler words, it means that you keep thinking about different aspects of a situation that you deem upsetting.

Think Of Your Tendencies

When you get upset by something, do you mull on it and keep going over the problem again and again? If yes, you are a ruminator too. Rumination is a wrecker of relationships. It is something that prevents you from letting go of minor mistakes that your partner has made and lets you hold on to them for a long duration of time. The thoughts keep cycling in your head and either make you distant from your partner or gives rise to an argument. Either way, the quality of the relationship suffers.

A lot of people who are in miserable relationships blame rumination as their biggest problems. These individuals cannot move on from the mistakes and negatives they encountered in the past. Because they choose not to let go of these thoughts, they are unable to move on and focus on their present. As a result, conflicts arise in their relationships, which leads to more ruminations. This way, the cycle continues.

Tips To Stop Ruminating

Once you get into the vicious cycle of rumination, it can be increasingly difficult to get out of it. If you have already entered the cycle, it is important to get out of it as quickly as possible.

The following are some tips to let go of your obsessive thoughts and break the cycle of rumination once and for all.

Distract Yourself

Whenever you feel like you are about to ruminate, find a distraction to break this cycle. Look around you and decide on an activity to do. You can do one of the following activities to distract yourself immediately:

- Call a friend or family member

- Watch a movie

- Do any pending chores

- Take a stroll in the neighborhood

- Read a book

Plan To Take Action

Instead of repeating the same negative thoughts again and again, use that thought to come up with a plan. Then, you can take action to address it. Inside your head, outline every single step you need to take to solve the problem. Or you can also write down your action plan on a piece of paper. Try being specific and set realistic expectations.

Once you start doing this, you will successfully interrupt your rumination process and move away from the negative thoughts.

Take Action

Following the last step, you must have come up with an action plan to sort out your ruminating thoughts. Now, you must make efforts to apply the plan in practical life. Take small steps until you put your mind to ease.

Question Your Thoughts

It is common to ruminate when you think you have made a major mistake. The same can occur when something traumatic occurs that you feel you are responsible for. If you start ruminating about a troubling thought, try putting this thought into perspective. Think about how this thought is not the best way to help you overcome your problems. Realize you need to do something, in reality, to get your problems sorted instead of constantly thinking about it.

Work On Enhancing Your Self-Esteem

Low self-esteem is often responsible for overthinking. Most people who ruminate are the ones that have problems with their self-esteem. Many studies have reported that a lack of self-esteem can lead to increased rumination. [6]

So, one way to stop rumination is to enhance self-esteem. For example, you can start building on existing strengths, which can give you a sense of mastery. This, in turn, can improve self-esteem.

Try Meditation

Meditation has proven to decrease rumination because it can clear your mind and help you achieve an emotionally calm state. So, when you find yourself in a repeated loop of thoughts, get to a quiet space and meditate.

Understand Your Triggers

Every time you start ruminating, try making a mental note of the situation that you are currently in. This means thinking about where you are, the time, and who else is with you. Once you have noted these triggers, try avoiding them as much as you can.

Talk To A Friend

Ruminating thoughts might make you feel isolated. Talking about these thoughts with a friend can help you break the cycle. The friend carries an external perspective and can help you share this perspective instead of ruminating with you.

Worrying About The Future

Whether you are in a long-term commitment or just a few days into your new relationship, it is common to worry about the future. This worry may have multiple origins but is normally due to the uncertainty.[7] It might also be the lack of trust, questions regarding the compatibility, or the fear of abandonment. For some people, this worry even occurs while stressing over the non-reciprocated feelings. No matter what the reason is, many people experience unease about the future of their relationship.

The real issue generates when this casual worry turns

into debilitating stress, which leads to self-sabotage. Ultimately, the relationship suffers.

Some common stressors that may cause you to worry about the future in a relationship include:

- The fear that your partner may cheat.

- The fear that your partner may break up with you.

- The feeling that you may not be good enough for your partner.

- The feeling that your partner may not be the one for you.

- The fear that the family or friends of your partner may not approve of you.

- The fear that your partner may choose other people over you.

Remember that worry and rumination might overlap, but they are psychologically different from each other. Whatever the reason behind your worry might be, it can destroy you and the relationship with your loved one.[8] So before it occurs, you must fix it with the help of the following tips.

Practice Vulnerability In Stages

A true relationship means letting someone in your life and granting them access to the parts of you that you hide from the world. When you worry too much about the future, you may feel like doing this is exposing the messier side of yourself.

Avoid falling prey to this kind of thinking. Remember that if your partner loves you, they will love all sides of you. Moreover, you do not have to share all of your deepest feelings. Keep experimenting with tiny exposures whenever you try to be vulnerable with your partner.

Communicate Your Expectations

Every single person who worries too much about the future naturally develops various thought loops. These repetitive thoughts keep coming back, and it almost seems impossible to get rid of them even if they seem silly. Moreover, these feelings and thoughts are extremely damaging to your relationship, as well.

For instance, if your partner does not call you after work for a few days like they normally do, you will be stuck in a thought loop. You will think that maybe they have gotten bored of you, or maybe they found a better alternative than you. Your mind keeps encountering these thoughts again and again when the real reason is that they are just busy with a project.

In such situations, the best thing to do is to communicate your expectations. It is not okay to constantly ask for reassurance from your partner, but now and then is fine. You can simply tell them that you look forward to their calls after work, and they mean a lot to you. Chances are your partner will acknowledge it and clear all your doubts.

Separate Your "Anxious Self" From Your "True Self"

Every person in a relationship has two sides: the anxious, worrying self and the true self. Your worrying self may mislead you into believing that if you open up to your partner about your worry, they may leave you.

These pessimistic thoughts occur because your constant worry about the future of your relationship has given you anxiety. When you suffer from anxiety, your mind makes all types of scenarios, most of which are not even close to reality. To combat this problem, speaking using your true self is a genuine solution. Give your true self a chance, and you may get an answer like "getting therapy does not label you as crazy. It means you are taking steps to become a greater version of yourself."

Accept That You Can't Control Everything Your Partner Does

A part of managing your worrisome thoughts regarding the future of your relationship includes letting go of things that are out of your hands. For example, your partner may have certain habits that annoy you. But you must bear in mind that you may not influence most of these habits.

Consider a scenario in which your partner likes to spend half of their Sundays playing soccer with their colleagues. You get frustrated but cannot do anything that threatens their autonomy in the relationship.

Your worry may urge you to control this situation, but the fact is this is something that you have no control on. You can most certainly communicate your wishes to them, but you cannot force them to base their decision on your ideas.

Remember, just because you worry about your relationship's future, you cannot snatch away your partner's individuality. It is only going to make things worse.

Talk About Your Worries And How You Tend To Express Them

Your worries regarding your relationships are not only yours to fight. You have the option to express them to your partner and see how that turns out.

While it is in your hands to find out the best of relaxation, you can make your partner an ally who can help you calm down when things get stressful. Sometimes, worries tend to increase when you try to cover it up because you are afraid of how others will respond to them. So, it is a better option to be open about how the future of your relationship worries you. Your partner may come up with a solution that ends those worries forever.

Create Some Rules Of Engagement For Arguments

It is normal for couples to argue, but the aftermath of these arguments can be worrisome for people who overthink. Suppose you get into a fight, and your partner eventually decides to walk away. While this act may annoy most people, overthinkers get a tough time in particular because walking away gives them uncertainty, which generates worry.

To end this kind of worry, set some ground rules regarding arguments. For example, you can set a rule that you may have a heated discussion only when you are ready to normalize after 24 hours. Both individuals can decide the rules in advance so that things turn out fine and without any worry after every argument.

Overthinking And Anxiety

Anxiety and overthinking are evil partners. The tendency to overthink is a hallmark of anxiety disorder. The anxious brain becomes hypervigilant and is always on the lookout for anything that seems worrisome or dangerous. It is common to label people who overthink a lot like the ones who generate problems when there aren't any. However, the reality is, for such people, problems do exist even when the rest of the world is unable to see it. Why? Because they suffer from anxiety side by side with their overthinking problem. When these culprits combine, the results come forward in the form of issues and problems that the rest are unable to see.

How Are Anxiety And Overthinking Connected?

Overthinking and anxiety go side by side. Any type of anxiety leads to overthinking, and overthinking, in turn, generates more anxiety. [9] There are some common themes that you can spot in the way anxiety causes overthinking.

For example:

- You obsess over what you could or should have said or did or didn't say in the past incidents.

- You worry about who you are and how you measure up to the world.

- You create scary what-if scenarios about all the things that could go wrong with you or your partner.

- You create the wildest consequences of your imagined incompetency and fault.

- You carry a fear of having a panic attack in a public place and are not willing to leave your home because of this reason.

- You worry about the multiple obsessive, scary thoughts and keep thinking about them non-stop.

- You keep thinking and cycling worries and vague thoughts that scare you.

The Marks Anxiety Can Leave On You

There are two ways in which anxiety secondary to overthinking can affect you. It may either make you dependent or completely avoidant. Let's discuss both personalities one by one.

Dependent

The dependent personality often results due to anxiety. In such people, anxious feelings make them nervous about being alone or handling certain conditions on their own.[10] These thoughts may also make them doubt every decision they make and every step they take. This suspicion ultimately leads to overdependence on others.

This dependent attitude can exhibit further characteristics like:

It Can Cause An Increase In Aggression

The kind of dependency that comes with anxiety can stimulate a greater degree of aggression. The constant need for support and care from a dependent person may lead to intimidation, violence, and abusive behavior.

Consider a jealous man who constantly abuses his wife. He might likely be displaying a dependency of this type. According to the experts, dependent men are at risk of becoming abusive when they fear that their partner is about to leave them.

It May Cause Codependency

Codependency is a phenomenon in which you lose sight of your own life because you focus too much on someone else's. It is common for a dependent, anxious person to become codependent and try controlling and managing the life of their partner. This leads to an imbalance which is extremely unhealthy for the relationship.

It May Create Fear Of Rejection

Anxious people who display dependent characteristics also have a fear of rejection deeply rooted within them. Such people are so habitual of their partners that they thought that their partner might reject them shakes them to the core.

It Gives Rise To An Excessive Need For Communication

Overdependence often leads to overthinking in social interactions too. Such overthinking may cause people to worry a lot when they do not get quick responses from their loved ones.

Therefore, people who are overly dependent on relationships are always struggling when it comes to communication. Some of them may even lash out in destructive ways when they feel like they are not getting enough communication from their partner.

Avoidant

Overthinking and anxiety can also lead to the development of avoidant behaviors.[11] For most people living with overthinking and anxiety, isolation is the only way to cope. Just like people who suffer from migraines make themselves distant from the external stimuli, people with anxiety also remove themselves from all relational stimuli.

Whenever such people feel stressed, they draw into self. With time, this habit becomes so strong that they forget how to express emotions. Due to this lack of expression, the partners of such people suffer.

Inability To Be Vulnerable

Have you ever felt terrified to tell your partner how much you need their support or help? Or have you ever avoided discussing an issue with them because you did not want to seem unlovable or inadequate? If yes, you are an avoidant. Avoidant people find it hard to be vulnerable. They think showing their neediness and weaknesses to their partner will make them unlovable in their eyes. They fear that if they express too much, they might face rejection in the hands of their better half. Due to this cycle of thoughts, they condition themselves to become invulnerable.

Uncomfortable In Romantic Relationships

Another common side effect of being an avoidant is a lack of an intimate relationship. Such people usually fail to get into relationships and to form an emotional bond with others. Even if they do manage to form an intimate connection, maintaining it becomes a real challenge. To protect themselves from rejection, avoidant people fear opening up to their partner. This lack of openness may make their partner develop feelings of rejection as well. Avoidant people also fear judgment and hence, wall off several parts of themselves even from their partners.

A study in the Journal of Personality Disorders has even proven that avoidant partners may develop negative emotions with success in romantic relationships.[12]

Tips To Overcome Anxiety Rooted In Overthinking

Overthinking and anxiety can make any relationship hard. However, it is possible to control these factors to give your relationship another chance. To accomplish this, consider the following tips.

Focus On How You Feel Instead Of Assessing The Relationship

If you think anxiety and overthinking are taking over you, take a pause and look at the situation closely. It might be because you are overthinking about your relationship while you must worry about how you "feel" about it or your partner. So, make it a practice to ask yourself how you feel about yourself in context with your relationship. Doing this will help you gain a better gauge of your position instead of making you analyze everything about your relationship.

Recognize Your Triggers

There is always some reason behind overthinking and feeling anxious about your relationship. What you must do is find that reason and remove it from your mind and sight whenever you feel threatened. For example, if the frequent lateness of your partner from work is what sets off anxiety in your case, try distracting yourself from these thoughts. In other circumstances, it might be because you feel that your marital quality is getting poorer. [13]

Whenever you feel like your mind is about to overthink about how your partner is purposely avoiding you by coming late, get busy. Start doing some house chore or simply tune in some soothing music. You can also use the power of argument to negate these thoughts. For example, you can conduct a dialogue with yourself where you defy these thoughts and calm yourself by thinking that your partner might just be busy with some project, or there might be too much traffic.

Practice Patience

Patience is the key to almost every achievement. To gain success, be it in your office or at home, you need to practice as much patience as possible. Even if the relationship is not going as you have imagined and you have hit a rocky road, calm down. Keep reminding yourself that bad days come in everyone's life, and they are certainly not there to stay.

Without patience, you are more likely to project this overthinking on your partner and fuel frequent arguments. These arguments will only harm you and your relationship.

Catch Yourself When You Start Looking For Hidden Meanings

In a relationship shadowed by clouds of anxiety and overthinking, it is not uncommon for people to avoid proper communication. People in such relationships usually avoid saying things that they truly feel and believe, and this can create a lot of trouble. Just because your partner is not fond of PDA and does not say I love you now and then, you may start looking for hidden meanings. You may feel like they don't love you anymore, or they don't want to be with you.

Similarly, if your partner casually tells you how you have gained a few pounds, you may start thinking that they now find you ugly and fat and want a new partner. Whenever you find yourself looking for hidden meanings in usual conversations with your partner, stop right there! It's not right, and doing this will only cultivate negativity in your heart regarding your partner. Soon, you will be obsessing over these thoughts and cause more anxiety. The cycle will keep on going until you destroy your entire relationship.

...erthinking Lead To ...curities?

"I am worried that my insecurities are getting between my relationship. Sometimes, I think that I am extra baggage. I am unable to get anything right, I am not good enough, and I never will be. None of this is because my partner has said or done something. It is purely my issue.

The scariest thing is that these insecurities are growing with time, and I have no idea how to conquer them. I am worried that they will destroy my relationship too. I often bring up petty issues and minor problems with other girls. I know how these issues are ridiculous because my partner is faithful, and I trust him. But at the same time, I keep getting these thoughts, I feel jealous, and I feel like I need constant validation from him."

Does this story sound familiar? Is it even remotely close to your relationship? If yes, you are destroying your relationship with overthinking and insecurities.

Insecurities Caused By Overthinking

Overthinking, in any relationship, fills your mind with all sorts of ideas. You know how a lot of them are silly and never going to prove true, yet your mind seems to keep fabricating them non-stop. As a result, many insecurities stem from the relationship that starts weakening the core.[14]

Jealousy

Jealousy refers to the feeling that someone may take what is yours. For instance, your spouse may become close to an attractive colleague, and this may make you feel jealous and threatened at the same time. Jealous behaviors are extremely common in relationships and can be dangerous and harmful. The jealous partner is, in fact, a needy person who is looking for constant reassurance that they are the one and no can replace them. At its worst, jealous behavior may exhibit itself in the form of distrustful and controlling behavior. Sometimes, these feelings may translate into emotional or even physical abuse.

A jealous person may try controlling the actions of their partner and keep checking their whereabouts. They may try to monitor the emails, texts, and calls too. This behavior can give rise to a pattern of distrust that is extremely unhealthy and may cause the relationship to fail. Respect and trust form the basis of every happy and healthy relationship. A person who struggles with jealousy is not able to trust their partner or respect them and their boundaries.

Such behavior can destroy the love and affection of every relationship over time. It may also give rise to repeated arguments and the constant need to prove themselves. Such relationships fail to thrive and can exhaust both partners, ultimately leading to separation.

Inadequacy

Have you ever questioned if you are good enough for your partner? Have you ever thought that the way you dress, speak, or live your life, in general, is not according to your partner's liking? If these questions have ever popped in your mind, you might be suffering from inadequacy. The feeling of inadequacy forces you to constantly evaluate if everything you do is according to your partner's wishes. You consistently look for their approval and make sure every single action you take is as per their liking.

If you have experienced abuse in the past, it does not matter what kind of abuse it was; it is common to feel inadequate. Feelings of inadequacy can often lead to insecurities as you continue to prove to yourself that you are not good enough for your partner and are irreplaceable.

Self-Consciousness

Two people in a relationship spend so much time together that they start taking each other's impact on the way they perceive themselves. Sometimes, this effect is positive since both of them understand and support each other. However, certain habits can have the opposite effect. For example, if a husband constantly teases his wife about how loud she is, she automatically takes the impact and considers herself unwanted. She will eventually develop feelings of insecurity in her relationship. To make up for this insecurity, she will remain self-conscious around her husband and try her best to hide her "flaw" in his presence.

Trust Issues

Trust means putting your confidence in something or someone. It is a fundamental experience that every human goes through. The feelings of trust play an important role in determining your happiness. Without trust, fear will rule.[15] Factors like overthinking in a relationship can shatter this trust and shake the very foundation on which it stands. When a person overthinks, they imagine all kinds of scenarios, no matter how unreal and unlikely to happen they are. These scenarios create insecurities, and insecurities give rise to trust issues. It is pretty clear that without trust, no relationship can work out.

Eight Steps To Free Yourself Of Insecurities Stemmed From Overthinking

Overthinking may lead to insecurities and wreak havoc in your relationship. But with the right tips and tricks, it is possible to get this situation under control.

Review Potential Causes

All relationships have their peaks and troughs. In a complicated relationship, arguments are common and can flare up at any time with no chance of resolution.

In such cases, it is not uncommon for partners to rethink their relationship. However, you must also remember that issues arise in every relationship from time to time, and you must work to resolve these hiccups gently. Insecurity and overthinking in relationships often have a problem at the back end, such as jealousy, fear, doubt, or money. Your first tip is to get to the bottom of whatever is leading to the generation of these feelings. Without learning about the root cause, you cannot possibly get to a solution.

Avoid Jumping To Conclusions

Prepare your mind to admit that the problem behind your insecurity can be imaginary and a result of excessive overthinking. Be as realistic as you can, and try sensing and reading your partner. If you still have doubts, be proactive and communicate them to your partner. Do not simply jump to conclusions and assume the worst on your own. Apply this rule whenever your partner is expressing their feelings to you. Try being receptive and open to what they say and do not jump to conclusions without understanding what they are conveying.

Accept There Are No Perfect Relationships

Every relationship has its challenges and hardships. It is extremely unlikely of you to share the same emotional state or mindset as that of your partner. So naturally, you will have disagreements. But these disagreements do not necessarily indicate that your relationship is unhealthy or in trouble.

Recognize Every Relationship Is Different

Having a troublesome relationship in the past can make you doubt and mistrust your current partner. However, you must realize that every relationship is unique. If your ex-partner has hurt you, it does not mean you should expect the same from your current one. Avoid creating insecurities in your current relationship just because you had them in your last one. Keep reminding yourself that your partner is a completely different person with their attributes and motivations. So, if you think you are holding on to beliefs formed in a previous relationship that can cause insecurities in your current one, let it go.

Affirm The Positives

It is common for partners to sometimes focus so much on the negatives that they completely forget about the positive attributes of their better halves. Instead of getting lost in the negatives, take out time to celebrate all the good things you enjoy in your relationship. Express what you love about your partner the most and explain the things they do that mean a lot to you. Focusing on the positives can increase the sense of security, and live the love your partner and you share.

Seek Security In Yourself

You can use your very own self-confidence to tackle any insecurity in your relationship. Instead of giving all the responsibility of your happiness to your partner, you can keep some of it and be self-assured. This may lighten the pressure on your partner and reduce the relationship tension too.

Connect With Your Partner

Try to communicate and reconnect with your partner to ease your insecurity. If you are facing hardships in your relationship, one way to overcome them is to take a new start. Get rid of all the previous perceptions and emotions. Start dating each other as if you have just met. This way, you can work together to build trust. Connecting with your partner also indicates exchanging the needs. So, sit down with them and talk about what both of you need from this relationship. Make your lists and try your best to check all the points on those lists.

If you are thinking of reconnecting with your partner, physical affection is also an important component. Small gestures like holding hands or randomly touching your partner's face can create affection and strengthen your bond.

Target Your Anxiety

To control your overthinking and insecurities, you must learn to tame your anxiety. For this purpose, daily meditation is the best solution. Exercise daily, take frequent time-outs, and try breathing exercises to control your anxiety levels. Moreover, you must focus on the hours of sleep you get every day in addition to the sleep quality. Try different anxiety-busting methods and figure out what works best for you.

Self-Centered Thinking In A Relationship

Imagine the following scenario:

You are in a relationship for the past few months. You suddenly begin to notice that your new boyfriend is spending a lot of time talking about himself and his life accomplishments.

Or

Your pretty new girlfriend is suddenly so full of herself that whenever she enters a room, she waits for heads to turn. Whenever you try to share an exciting event or a recent success you achieved, she fails to acknowledge it. All of a sudden, the conversation takes a turn and focuses on their achievements and adventures.

If one of these scenarios describes you or your partner, you are experiencing self-centered thinking.

What Is Self-Centered Thinking, And How It Affects Your Relationships?

Self-centered thinking is a pattern of thinking in which you only care about yourself and nothing else. [16] Your partner, your relationship, and the bond you share mean nothing to you. But how does overthink lead to self-centered thinking?

Through Excessive Anxiety

It is common for anxious people to overthink all the time. Thoughts like the following commonly cross their minds no matter where they are.

"Did I upset them? Oh no, I think I must have. They did not reply to me for five minutes. I am a horrible partner and person. They will certainly leave me."

"Did I do this correctly? If it goes wrong, my partner will consider me a failure. Why haven't I been more careful before?"

"I am panicking. But why is this happening to me? Everything was fine. Maybe it's just the way I am. I don't deserve to be in any relationship."

When you are anxious, you become lost in your thoughts and start fighting an extremely distracting battle. This battle does not let you focus on the outside world. It's not that you don't care about anything else but that you are so busy fighting the battles that you fail to do so.

With so much worry and tumult inside your brain, you create an emotional storm, which makes it hard to remember anything other than yourself. It would not be uncommon in these circumstances to forget that your partner has a late-night meeting. It would also not be surprising if you do not remember their promotion day even though they have reminded you five times already.[17] Such situations are frustrating for both partners and can be a real challenge to overcome.

Through Feelings Of Inadequacy

People with self-centered thinking in their relationships generally have feelings of inadequacy inside them. Selfish lovers mostly have something to hide, and they fear that if they give those secrets up, it will reveal their flaws. These selfish lovers fail to realize that such a pattern of thinking will only damage their relationship.

When you are too involved in yourself due to self-centered thinking, you fail to notice the problems and struggles of your partner. For example, you may only think about your tough routine when your partner is standing right in front of your eyes juggling with three jobs.

This problem can create distances between the two partners and weaken their love. When you are so focused on your issues, you cannot be there to help others. This includes you never being truly available to help your partner out when they need you. Your partner might be asking you to help find their important documents while you just stand there thinking about how your presentation will go tomorrow.

This automatically makes your partner feel like you do not care about them. Insecurities and mistrust will develop and wreak the relationship.

Changing The Center Of Your Thinking

Self-centered thinking stands in the way of bonding with another person, even when you love them. It creates hurdles every step of the way, which makes it difficult to maintain any relationship. Therefore, it is important to remove such a pattern of thinking as soon as you can. For this purpose, the following tips may work.

Get To The Root Cause

Sometimes, people become self-centered because of a certain experience of the past. So, before you completely dismiss them because of their selfishness, try getting to the reason behind this pattern of thinking. Getting to the root cause first and understanding it does not mean that you must let your partner go off the hook. Instead, it pushes you to discover what triggers such a thinking pattern so that you can control it and make it less powerful. This tip works for both selfish and selfless partners.

Let Them Speak

Whenever your partner is saying something, try not to interrupt them. If you interrupt them in the middle or throw your tantrums instead of listening to them, your partner may not be able to speak their heart out. This act may seem selfish on your part and make you a self-centered person. So, try listening to the other person once in a while to promote good communication.

Pay Attention

Sometimes, you think you are giving enough attention to your better half. However, there is a lot more depth than you can ever imagine. [18] Try to concentrate on every little thing your partner has to say. If they are upset because of something, do not take it for granted or just rub it off. Make them realize that you understand them, you are listening to them, and are there to help them. Remember, it is not always about you.

Remember The Happy Times

This tip is for both partners, irrespective of who the self-centered person is. Why should you only focus on the miserable stuff and memories when you share a lot of happiness too? You have been growing together ever since you came into a relationship and must have shared many happy moments. Remember them and rejoice in them.

Set Some Boundaries

There is always a delicate line between seeking attention and getting on the other person's nerves. Your partner might be doing their best to tolerate you and your self-centered thinking, so you must not push it. Notice when you are overdoing it and step back on your own.

Evaluate Yourself As A Partner

Ask yourself if you would like to get into a relationship with yourself? Would you be able to tolerate a person who is exactly like you, with the same thinking and actions? Would you ever be able to love yourself if you were another person? If the answer is no, evaluate yourself. Find out the characteristics that make you unwanted in your own eyes and fix them.

Overthinking In Long-Distance Relationships

"Is he/she worth the wait?"

"Do they feel the same way as I do?"

"Am I kidding myself if I think this can work?"

"Shouldn't I just date the mailman? At least I would get to see them every day."

"Does my boyfriend even exist? Or is it all just a scam?"

Long-distance relationships suck. There isn't a single person who has ever said, "Yeah, my partner lives 6000 miles away from me in Finland. It's going great." On the contrary, every person you will meet in a long-distance relationship will have this agonizing feeling.

It's like someone is carving out their heart using a butter knife and replacing it with blinking chat windows and unsatisfactory video calls.

Consider the story of John, a young, handsome guy who got into long-distance relationships twice. The first time he got in a long-distance relationship, both he and his girlfriend tried their best to make things work. However, things fell apart and never got to be the same, mostly because both of them were immature and too young to handle the distance.

In his second relationship, both John and his girlfriend agreed that their lives were leading them to different areas of the world. So, it was better if they let each other go than keep struggling. Nevertheless, they still tried to continue their relationship for one more year, which turned out to be the worst one of all. So, they quietly split later.

The third time, John was wise enough to plan with his

girlfriend and end their distance as soon as possible. Both of them made the necessary sacrifices for it too. Six months into moving together, they got married.

While John's long-distance relationship had a happy ending, it does not happen in every case. Not every couple can immediately move in together, so they somehow have to manage to live with thousands of miles separating us. In such circumstances, it is not surprising if one or both of the partners develop patterns of overthinking.

What Can You Do About It?

Long-distance relationships rarely work out. But why? Mostly, it is because couples are not able to see or meet each other frequently, which causes them to imagine all kinds of scenarios in their minds. [19] The following are some additional reasons why long-distance relationships can lead to overthinking.

Your Time Together

Most people in long-distance relationships commonly report the feeling as if they are losing their minds. Their happiness and life revolve around when they are going to see their partner next. They forget how to live and function as a single person, even if they have been single their whole life.

For such people, their entire day revolves around staring at their phones, waiting for a text from their partners. At night, they are anxiously waiting for a video call. This lifestyle is extremely unhealthy, especially if they are already a patient of anxiety and depression, and can easily lead to overthinking.

Especially during the initial days of the relationship, it becomes really hard to find the right balance between your life and your relationship.

Communication And Miscommunication

Misunderstandings and miscommunications are common in relationships. They occur when you are sharing a house with your partner. They occur with a much higher frequency when you are miles apart and talk to each other via text messages and phone calls. Consider the following example to understand how long-distance relationships create miscommunication.

During the initial days of the relationship, Jane's three consecutive emails to her partner Mike ended up in his junk folder. Lucky for her, Mike was not the type of guy who would get easily offended and stop writing to her just because she had done the same. Days passed, and they never got to know what happened. But if it was someone more sensitive, that could mean the end of a relationship.

Another time, both partners were talking over text messages when Jane expressed something she worried about. To this, Mike responded as "that's a fair concern."

What Jane interpreted from this answer was that Mike is trying to say that she must be worried about this. While this response was highly unsettling for Jane, she kept discussing the matter with Mike. Only minutes later, she realized that what Mike was trying to say was, "I understand what you are worried about, but that will not happen." So, you see, Mike was trying to be supportive, but because conversations over texts are not predictable, it can easily turn into miscommunication.

When you are a part of long-distance relationships, accessing non-verbal cues like body language, eye contact, voice tone, and facial expressions can be hard. Without these cues, it is very much possible to misjudge when someone is joking or being serious too, which makes communication harder. [20]

Security

It is common to feel insecure in a relationship at some point in life. Everyone has moments when they feel inadequate or threatened too. These are the times when worries and fears run away on you, and you get anxious. Everyone hit low points and have bad days too. Remember that this is completely normal, and is a part of the give and take in relationships.

However, if these feelings of insecurity become chronic, it depicts a bigger problem and can even take a toll on the relationship. In long-distance relationships, it is quite common to develop chronic insecurity since you are not with your partner and not aware of what they are doing at a particular moment. As a result, all kinds of insecurities arise in your mind that make you question their love, trust, and even loyalty.

The Fear Of Growing Apart

If your partner moves to another city or country and pauses or slows down some aspects of the relationship, the rest of your life does not stop. You do not stop learning, changing, and growing just because the person you love is not with you daily. The same goes for them. Both of you are just accumulating experiences, some of which will change you.

When you are a part of a long-distance relationship, it becomes harder to identify how your partner is accepting this change. You are also unable to track this process of change in them. This fear of not knowing can slowly drift you into thinking if your partner wants you some time from now. You will also try to overthink if you will be able to adjust with them after such a long time.

Physical Intimacy

Another way distance can affect both partners in long-term relationships is a lack of physical intimacy. These partners may face trouble managing this intimacy, as meeting each other more frequently is not possible, given the distance. A lack of physical intimacy occurs, which puts both of them in a dilemma if they must satisfy their sexual needs in other ways. Even if the partners decide to turn to other ways, most of them feel disappointed for resorting to them even though they are in a happy relationship. They feel frustrated. After all, they can't begin a sexual relationship with people around them because they are committed to someone living far away from them. All these things pile up and make the partners wonder if their long-term relationship is even worth all this struggle or if they should just end it right here.

Ways Overthinking Impacts Your Relationships

Now that you know how common it is to overthink in long-term relationships, let's move on to different ways overthinking can impact your relationships.

Creates More Anxiety

Anxiety is not something easy to live with, especially when it is due to long-term relationships. It is not good for you as well as the people who are close to you, including your partner, family, and friends. A lot is going on in your mind when you are anxious. Most of the thoughts you encounter consist of hypothetical situations, which may or may not be true. Yet, they will continue to cross your mind anyway.

You feel like you are always at the edge, always wondering what's going to happen next. You may also get this unsettling feeling that you are completely unaware of what's coming next. The distance between you and your partner makes the situation harder as you find yourself in a loop of multiple what-ifs. If, at the same time, your partner is suffering from anxiety, that makes it a completely difficult and even harder story to bear. Sometimes, there are moments of complete silence, while at other times, you are getting anxiety attacks.

Create More Insecurities

Every human being wishes always to know where their partner is and what they are doing. This feeling of insecurity and possessiveness is hard to overcome, especially in long-term relationships. You often start panicking when your partner does not reply within a few minutes. The distance between you makes trusting difficult and increases possessiveness. This feeling of insecurity for a long time can hurt you as well as your relationship. The situation for your partner is no different as they constantly have to prove their loyalty to ease your insecurities.

Can Cause You To Question Or Integrate Your Partner

Research suggests that negativity is one of the primary factors that lead to the termination of long-term relationships. If there is a steady stream of negativity in your relationship, it fails to thrive. For long-term relationships, it is quite easy to get lost in the negative aspects. You feel alone all the time, constantly miss each other, and when your partner fails to give you attention for some reason, you start interrogating them. You interrogate them on the slightest inconveniences and suspicions that arise in your mind. This constant interrogation further boosts negativity and can even affect one or both of you physically. Your brain activity reduces, and your immune system weakens. Your intelligence also decreases, and your overall quality of life suffers.

Can Cause Mistrust

When you are in a long-distance relationship, you are not able to see the other person all the time. So, it can get really hard to find out what's going on with them via text messages and calls only. For example, you may get upset and overthink you have hurt your partner when they send you "K" instead of "OK." Such type of miscommunications can commonly occur in long-term relationships

Can Lead To Jealousy

The famous proverb "out of sight, out of mind" continues to create a sense of jealousy in long-term relationships, even today. Even if you are not the jealous type of person, a long-distance relationship may bring out your insecurities and make you one. Every relationship has its moments of insecurity, especially during the initial days, when you are getting to know your partner. When your partner lives far away from you, you need to reign in these insecurities and be open about them instead of keeping them bottled up. Unfortunately, this expression of insecurities is quite hard for most people, and they usually avoid doing so. As a result, feelings of jealousy begin to generate. These feelings of jealousy are not necessarily because your partner is hanging out with another someone who can potentially replace you. As a girl, you can even feel jealous when your long-term relationship partner goes out to play some soccer with his guy friends. You get jealous because his friends go to spend time with them while you sit there waiting for your next plan of meeting up.

Stopping Overthinking In A Long-Distance Relationship: What Can You Do?

By now, you must be clear that overthinking is a potential destroyer of long-distance relationships. So, you must avoid practicing it as much as you can. For this purpose, the following tips can be useful.

Don't Bottle Up Your Emotions

Being in a long-distance relationship means you are in an emotional roller coaster. Sometimes, there are high highs, and sometimes, you hit the low lows. A relationship of any type can generate a lot of feelings in you. You need to find a way to channel these thoughts. If you keep bottling them up, you are going to explode someday, and it is not going to be a pretty sight.

So, whether it is a trusted friend, a family member, a journal, or even a therapist, let go of your emotions. Take care not to bottle your feelings regarding your partner. If something about them is bothering you, be straight forward and tell them at once. Just like any relationship, you must not keep waiting unless you reach your last straw and give voice to your concerns.

Improve Your Communication

Communication is a key factor when it comes to long-distance relationships. If you are not going to communicate with each other more often, many misconceptions and false assumptions will rise, which will further exacerbate your cycle of overthinking.[21] So always go the extra mile to make sure your communication is well. Try scheduling your calls in advance so that both of you have something to look forward to. Doing this will also add an element of excitement in your relationship. You will also spend less time wondering when you are going to talk to your partner next. If for some reason, one of you fails to make it at the appointed time, you wouldn't overthink when you get to talk to them again because you will know it already.

Stop Before You React

When you are living miles apart from the love of your life, it is understandable to become a little more sensitive because you are not an ordinary couple. So, in this state of heightened sensitivity, if you come across something your partner said or did that offends you, you may react spontaneously. Don't! You must remember that misunderstandings are a part of every relationship. They are a little more common in long-distance relationships than the other types. So, if something has occurred that's bothering you, you must calm yourself and think about it completely instead of blowing up right there.

Trusting your partner can significantly help apply this

concept. If you have faith in your partner, you must feel secure enough to let them go out and do what they wish to do. All this while knowing that they still love you and will only come back to you.

Join A Support Group

Feeling lonely is quite common in people with long-distance relationships. So, you must reach out for help, and what better way to get support than chatting with people in the same position as you? Many long-distance relationship groups and forums are working online and taking free joining. You can join any one of them and share your experiences and feelings. You can even ask for advice or give it to others. You may make friends who live nearby and can hang out with them too.

Learn To Write Out Your Negative Thoughts And Fears

Many people in long-distance relationships become

neurotic and overly critical to the point where every minor inconvenience is the potential end of their relationship. Such negative thoughts and fears are damaging to any relationship, and it is important to get rid of them as soon as possible. One way to do so is to take a piece of paper and write down all your fears, concerns, and thoughts regarding your relationships. Keep reminding yourself that by writing them down, you are getting it out of your system. Later, when your mind gets a little clearer, revisit your thoughts and negate them one by one.

Making A Long-Distance Relationship Last: Tips And Tricks To Follow

In addition to working on your habit of overthinking, you can also follow the following tips to make your long-distance relationship last longer.

Plan To See Each Other Regularly

Maintaining the delicate travel balance is an essential component of every long-distance relationship. How often do you pack up to see your partner, and how long is your usual stay? Many factors decide these two questions, for example, the time you can get off from work and your travel budget. The best and ideal practice is to visit each other every three weeks for at least two days. For most people, the hectic work schedule and budget concerns may not allow this. For them, a monthly or two-monthly meeting can suffice. However, make sure you never spend three months in a row without seeing each other as it only weakens the relationship.

Have Realistic Expectations

It is a good practice to be positive in your thinking and approach. However, you must make sure that you are realistic when it comes to long-distance relationships. For example, you may wish that your partner visits you every day, texts you day and night, and calls you every four hours. All these wishes are not harmful, but, at the same time, they are not realistic either. You must acknowledge that both you and your partner have your own lives at your places and may not always be available to give you the maximum time.

Another important aspect to consider realistically when it comes to long-distance relationships is the end goal. Do you want to stay at a distance forever? Of course not. You will have to discuss with each other the future of your relationship at some point. You may also achieve your goal of living together in the same area. However, if you fail to come to terms with a common goal regarding the future of both of you, it might be time to re-evaluate your relationship.

Talk About Your Fears

Some of you try hard not to express what's on your mind in fear that it may raise a conflict. The situation remains the same, even if it is something that you need to bring upfront and be straightforward with it.

Practicing this approach can weaken your long-distance relationship. Instead, you must try gauging when you feel the right time to talk about your fears and expectations about the relationship. Ensure that both of you know that these fears and expectations are a normal part of every relationship; be it long-distance or not.

Create an environment that is so secure that it encourages you and your partner to express their thoughts. When one of you does so, provide them comfort and reassurance and then go back to enjoying your time together. Don't dwell on your fears and expectations; most of them relate to your past or the future and not the present.

Have Hobbies Outside The Relationship

Look on the bright side: being in a long-distance relationship gives you time to do things that you truly enjoy without compromising on your partner. Think of all the fun activities you used to do when you were single? Maybe it is a good time to get back to painting, or re-joining the yoga class. You may even attempt to learn a brand new hobby.

The basic aim of this tip is to let you acquire something that you are passionate about. When you have something else to focus on other than your partner, you will build confidence and feel accomplished. At the same time, it will also give your partner space and peace of mind.

Don't Forget Your Other Relationships

One thing that commonly happens in relationships is that you start spending so much time with your partner that you completely forget about others. You start ignoring your family and friends, which can be damaging to your health. Luckily, you do not need to do this in a long-distance relationship because you will have enough time to give to everyone. So, utilize this opportunity and make the most of your time with family and friends. Plan out fun activities, maybe a getaway trip at the weekend, and have lots of fun. Don't forget to advise your partner to do the same.

Miscellaneous

The following are some miscellaneous activities you can do to strengthen your relationship with your partner.

Perform Online Activities

A great way to spend time with your partner is to play online games. You may also consider watching a documentary on online platforms at the same time. You may use video calls to conduct singing sessions or take a walk outside while you are on a video call.

Do Similar Things

Recommend different TV shows, music, movies, and books to each other. When you read, watch, and listen to some things, you will have more to talk about. This activity will also help you enjoy shared experiences even though you live miles apart.

Have A Goal In Mind

- "What do we wish to achieve at the end of the day?"

- "How long will we stay apart?"

- "What will happen in the future?"

These are some questions that you must ask yourselves. Decide on a common goal and stick to it.

Stay Honest With Each Other

Talk more often about your feelings of fear, jealousy, insecurity, apathy, etc. If you hide any of these things from your partner, the secret will come out sooner and later and prove destructive for the relationship. So, it is better, to be honest with each other from the start. Express your feelings and let your partner support you.

Controlling Overthinking Through Self-Awareness

In any instance, in time, it is very much possible for you to change the way you view a particular circumstance. Your merry thoughts could go all gloomy before you even know it. Imagine you're on your first date; it starts with you thinking about how excited you are to meet the person as you sit at the restaurant. Moments pass by, and you begin wondering why your date hasn't made it yet, and you turn to your phone to drop a message. Your messages go unanswered, and so do your calls. Now starts the overthinking. Your mind gushes with thoughts and insecurities, and you begin to question if you were simply not good enough. You wonder if anyone will ever like you for who you are, and you wonder why do you even try. This specific one is an easy example, given most of us can relate to being ghosted at some points in our life. The overthinking that follows and the belittling of oneself too, it's relatable. So are interpreting mere text messages and odd uses of emojis to draw bigger conclusions.

Likewise, overthinking inculcates itself in many more instances of your lives. The time you give yourself to reflect plays a great part in contributing to your mindfulness. It also allows you to be more aware of yourself. In turn, self-awareness gives way to progression and growth. Contrarily, the time you spend overthinking scenarios leads to the opposite. Overthinking fuels unproductive and belittling thoughts. In simpler words, overthinking entraps you in a vicious cycle of self-destruction.

Therefore, you mustn't let yourself remain trapped in the cycle. To do so, you can make some attempts. Firstly, create self-awareness.

What Is Self-Awareness?

The Self-Awareness Theory states that people are mere observers of their thoughts, rather than being the thoughts itself. It states that a person is a thinker, completely discreet from his/her thoughts. [22] Often, people tend to go through their days without stopping to bask and listen to the whispering thoughts in their heads. Though they are there, they aren't given much attention to and are acted upon by one's own will. Luring your attention to the hidden whispers of your head is a skill that the researchers Duval and Wicklund have called "self-evaluation."

When a person self-evaluates, it allows them to note their feelings and action and lets them ponder upon whether they should be feeling and acting the way they are. This action is comparing one's deed against a standard of one's rightness. Unknowingly, we indulge in this action daily to critique our thoughts and actions. The entire concept behind using standards to compare is to practice self-control. This practice is what helps us state right from wrong and aids us in making the correct decisions and, thus, accomplishing milestones.

The theory has been tested for its authenticity multiple times, given it came into being a considerable amount of time ago. Time has uncovered large amounts of information on self-awareness, its links, and its advantages. This information can allow people to improve self-awareness in themselves and others, too.

When you compare yourselves in light of your fixated standards, according to the theory, there are two results you can get:

1. You "pass", which essentially means that you find correlations between yourself and your fixed standards.

2. You "fail", which means that you do not completely resemble and live by your fixed standards.

Moving on, after you encounter dissimilarities between yourselves and your standards, you'll find yourself with two obvious options. Your first option will be to attempt to fill the void between yourself and your standards. On the other hand, your second option would be to disregard the dissimilarities completely.

The Self-Awareness Theory and a wide series of research have stated that there are multiple determining factors in play when a person begins to react to the situation. Chiefly, people's decisions revolve around what they make of the whole situation. If they believe that there's a stronger possibility of filling the void, they'll attempt to do so. However, if the void seems too big, people are more likely not to do anything about it. It's all a matter of their ease.

Additionally, how people react is also dependent on the amount of time and effort the correcting will take. The longer the process will take, and the larger the void is, the less likely an individual is to make efforts. In simpler words, when the void is assumed to be too big to fill, it eventually means that filling it will require determination and consistency. Because of the work it demands, individuals tend to refrain from self-evaluation wholly.

Additionally, another determining factor in a person opting to go through the struggle of filling their dissimilarities is dependent on their present self-awareness. Self-aware individuals are optimistic in thinking of excelling in all their endeavors. When a person has a high self-awareness, they tend to have high hopes as well. This adds to the possibility of them filling the voids between their practices and their standards.

Contrarily, it is equally possible that a self-aware person believes to be a lesser chance of them excelling. They might believe that their final decision takes more effect from the external contributing factors than their determination. This isn't completely wrong. Outer factors influence your success, but it is you who is the driving and determining force to determine whether you go uphill or downhill. Self-awareness allows you to:

Be Mindful Of Your Own Emotions

Self-consciousness is a vital aspect of gaining emotional intelligence. Developing emotional intelligence not only strengthens relationships but also allows you to do better to yourself. This is so because when you are mindful of your behaviors and can see the impact they have on others, you can use it to carry out a self-analysis to understand why you react the way you do.

Communicate Efficiently

Through knowing yourself and understanding the reasoning behind your actions, you will find it easier to express your happiness, your sorrow, your anger, and your dreams directly to your partner. When you speak out clearly, your listening partner will be able to understand you far better and see you for who you are.

Boost Optimism

Optimism grows when a person continues to see proof that after understanding themselves, every change they made to their lives gave into progression and growth. Maintaining persistence only brightens life further. With this, when the person notices that the possibility of a happier existence does exist, they make genuine efforts to work their way towards it.

With this newly formed optimism, you can refresh your relationship, and instead of viewing it negatively, you can focus on its positive aspects. Then, you can start working on these positive aspects to strengthen the bond and love you share with your partner.

Evaluate Yourself More Effectively

If your relationship is on the fall due to your habit of overthinking and overanalyzing everything, self-awareness can help you. With self-awareness, you will have more knowledge about your ideas and concepts, and using them; you can assess yourself whenever you feel like you are overthinking again. You can use the power of self-awareness to argue if the things that are bothering you are real or just a fabrication of your mind. With this newly achieved self-awareness, you can not only overcome these fabricated thoughts but use them to improve your life in the future.

To understand it in a better way, consider the following example:

Monique has issues with her boyfriend, Luis. She believes Luis doesn't appreciate her enough and fails to express his love for her even in the littlest ways. This often leads to them having heated arguments over the same issue. Suddenly she thinks she may be adding fuel to the fire.

She looks internally and knows she doesn't express Luis's gratitude. She also realizes that she often disregards the good bits and efforts Luis makes for her along with the little physical gestures expressing his affection.

Monique considers her thoughts when Luis loses a chance to make her feel good and realizes that she deliberately believes he stops doing the things she wants. She spends time reflecting and conversing with Luis, telling him how she wants to receive affection and respect. With it, they continue trying to build on and strengthen their relationship.

Be Increasingly Self-Assured

Confidence comes from being confident about one's self. If you tend to go through life constantly doubting yourself and your worth and not knowing what you aspire from life, you're likely to overthink and cause troubles unnecessarily. With confidence, feelings of insufficiency cease. The likelihood of you constantly belittling yourself for the silliest reasons ceases too. Thus, another root cause of overthinking gets off the list, which only leads to a much healthier and happier relationship.

Eight Ways To Improve Self-Awareness

Try Meditating

Meditating can be the best way to enhance self-awareness. This particular method improves your sense of self-awareness in a slow, progressive way. Mostly, the exercise revolves around simply inhaling and exhaling to calm your body down and allow your mind to wander into thoughts. The core idea here isn't to perform these as a ritual; sitting back in peace and contemplating over things as a routine does the trick too.

An idea could be practicing these breathing exercises a few minutes before you sleep. When you get in the zone, here's a few questions to ask yourself:

- What do I want out of this relationship?

- What am I contributing to this relationship?

- What is my contribution to taking this relationship downhill?

- What do I need to change?

Jot Down Aims, Strategies, And Priorities

Writing down what you want to do and monitoring how good you're doing is a great way to boost self-awareness. For one thing, Warren Buffet is known to carefully understand the reasons behind investing, when he's ready to make one. His journal entries act as a background record that lets him determine whether potential findings may or may not be due to sound judgment or just plain chance.

Inspired by Benjamin Franklin, find a pattern to pursue. Franklin has maintained a "balance sheet" of both his assets and liabilities. In diarizing any new skill, he felt he could gain from someone else, and by writing down any self-perceived shortcomings, he could better determine how his character's "net worth" had increased over time. So why not use it in your relationship? Take a piece of paper and write down all the goals and plans you wish to achieve in your relationship. Don't forget to include your partner in this tip and ask them to do the same. Now keep this piece of paper in front of your eyes all the time to remind yourself that you have all these things to achieve together.

Write Down Your Traits

You can always take personality tests to help you understand your dominant traits. There are plenty of these available online that can prove beneficial. However, keep in mind that there are no correct or incorrect answers to these tests. Instead, they force you to think about a collection of characteristics and features. Then it's up to you to identify which of those most closely associate with you.

Ask The Three 'Whys'

When you find yourself overthinking, ask yourself, "Why?" and when you have an answer to it, go with the same question again and again. You will have three reasons for your overthinking. If these reasons seem valid enough to you, you will know you're overthinking is not taking you on a toxic path. And eventually, when you do have a final answer to your problems, these three whys will also ensure you don't begin to overthink your final answer. Through this, you'll learn more about your driving force in the relationship with your partner. This is another key to heightening self-awareness.

Know What Others Think About You

As Carlson suggests, you can never really be aware of what others think of you.[23] To know, you need to turn to your friends and people who know you for gaining feedback. Your friends can be the ideal way to get feedback, and when seeking it, make sure they know you're looking for crystal clear answers. To do so, it is your job to make your friend feel safe enough to be going all candid with you.

Alternatively, when you catch yourself in the act, call your friends, and get their opinion on the situation which you may be exaggerating. For example, give them a call and say, "I know I often tend to exaggerate little details into making them bigger situations. Could you please remind me not to do that every time you either catch me doing it or I come confessing to you about it?"

Self-Reflect Occasionally

Self-reflect is extremely important. For this, you'll have to spare out some time from your busy routine to sit and reflect over how you have been with your partner. Correspondingly, look for ways you could improve. The more persistent you remain with this, the more you'll start to see.

Everyday self-reflection is not as complicated as the competitive businesses require. Despite the fewer and constant flow of knowledge through our portable devices, there is still a desire to do more.

Set aside 15 minutes per day because it takes time to self-reflect and considers writing your thoughts down; it's more efficient.

Look For Repeating Thoughts

Look at the general patterns of repetitive thinking. Will you criticize yourself or your friend much of the time? Would you believe your partner dismisses your successes as insignificant and unimportant?

The series of negative thoughts keep you entrapped, and the only way you break out of the cycle is through optimistic thoughts and self-love. This way, you gain more control over the auto-pilot carrying you around.

Acquire And Accept Constructive Feedback

Don't continuously ask yourself if you're doing well in

your relationship or not. Instead, questioning people who were close observers of your relationship is more fruitful. Ask them for their feedback on how they have observed you be and make sure they are honest with you when they disclose your entire plus and minus points. When you do receive feedback, don't get defensive of it. Accept it and work to better the pointed flaws. However, if you disagree with the feedback, think of it the way most people perceive you. And if you think you need to change that, work your way towards the change.

With this, you can bring an end to overthinking and take your self-awareness way high up. You'll now have the chance to refine yourself, your skills, and your principles. These will all work their way into healthy inputs from your sides in a relationship.

Controlling Negative Thoughts With Self-Reflection

One can never truly know if the person they are with is right for them. It doesn't matter if you've been with them for years or someday, it's always a wise decision to sit back and bask upon the kind of relationship you two share. Often, it's asking the deeper and scarier questions that help to make life-changing decisions. At the beginning of any relationship, people mostly tend to disregard certain red flags or unappealing qualities and make do with them. The reason behind this does not want to look for someone new all over again.

Speaking of longer relationships, people lose themselves within the bounds of comfort in them, and while doing so, stop questioning if their relationship holds the same importance within their life and still adds the same meaning as it did initially. When one finds oneself in the middle of these questions, self-reflection comes to the rescue to dodge the toxic phase of overthinking of whether it all even holds meaning.

What Is Self-Reflection?

Self-reflection is a route that takes you to the determination of yourself, things important to you, and how your mind processes everything. It doesn't matter what your current relationship status is, reflecting upon yourself is vital before committing to any relationship. It is only after identifying one's self and one's futuristic desires that one can determine what turns to make along the route in life.

Self-reflection can contribute immensely to your bond with your "other half." [24] Reflection may help you realize that you deserve better treatment and also expect better of yourself in treating others. Having figured situations out, you can converse with your partner over things that bother you and the changes you wish to see in yourself and them. By reflection and realization, you'll be able to stop the same unpleasant situations from reoccurring.

What Can Self-Reflection Add To Your Relationship?

While you waste time figuring if your partner treats you right or is honest, you overlook their strengths with their flaws. As a result, you will stop valuing them and treat them in a way they do not deserve. Hence, it is necessary you keep a check on this habit. The checks will contribute greatly to a better working and a happy relationship.

When you find yourself puzzled, here are a few questions you could ask yourself:

- Have you been undervaluing your relationship?

- Have you made him feel immature?

- How do you deal with arguments in your relationship?

- Did you value yourself?

- What do you mean by a perfect relationship?

- Have you been treating others the way you are expecting them to treat you?

- What could you do better about yourself to gain the lacking affection from your partner?

With constant self-reflection, you'll be able to figure out the lacing aspects in your relationship and then consequently, work on them. It will also develop a better understanding of your present relationship while making yourself more considerate of your partner's efforts as well. In simpler words, self-reflection is a means of evaluating yourself and correcting yourself to be a better person to your partners. It also allows you to fixate the ethics you want to live your life by.

Self-reflection also allows you to interpret what you feel and why you feel it. When you let thoughts take over your head, it leaves you in a state of never-ending confusion. This confusion makes it pretty hard to break from the toxic cycle. Jotting these clustered thoughts down on a notepad can help you get a clearer perspective of what you're feeling and why you're feeling it. When laid out in front of you, your feelings may seem a lot less complicated to interpret. The only way this ends is with you having a clearer idea and a solution at hand, and you'll find yourself on the way to devising a strategy to tackling your figured complications.

Overthinking causes you to presume your problems are by far greater than they may be. When you allow yourself to analyze situations calmly, you'll see that you already know most of the answers you're seeking.

Self-reflection also grants you the chance to mend the way you process situations. Mostly, people tend to ponder over the mistakes of their partners, such as the instances they took them for granted or embarrassed them around others. Therefore, when one jots all these incidents down, they must question themselves if they believe them to be true. They should question if their partner is always the only one really at fault while they always stand right. When they begin to ponder over these details, they'll realize that what they keep telling themselves about their own actions and attitude isn't always true.

Three Reflections To Get A Different Perspective

Pondering over the three reflections below can give you an idea about why you excessively and necessarily think. It may also prove effective in helping you find solutions.

What Are You Like As A Partner?

Would you want to date someone with the same qualities as yours? What qualities dominate you? Can you be controlling, obsessive, or idle? Are you more of a taker or a giver? Do you end up making mistakes most? If so, don't drown in guilt because you're not the only one making mistakes. In a relationship, one often looks out more for the mistakes of others than one's self. Hence, relationships go downhill when no one is reflecting upon themselves. For a relationship to thrive, you must look at yourself from your partner's eyes and make it up to them when you rightly fail to please them.

This surely doesn't mean both individuals need to be an embodiment of perfection. Instead, it means that relationships ask for loyalty and accountability from both. Another common and mistaken belief is that apologizing belittles one's self, which is wrong. Taking responsibility for your actions is a sign of strength, and loyalty implies self-value. It makes you a considerate person, and so, reflecting on ways you could add more to your relationship doesn't belittle but makes you heedful.

Do I See My Partner's Best Qualities?

You need to be honest with your partner, much like you need to be with yourself. Therefore, questions: do you focus on your partner's minuses more than their pluses? Do you manifest unnecessary doubts when all your partner is trying to do is satisfy you? Do you keep telling yourself that they can't do anything, right? The qualities that you see most in your partner, be it good ones or bad ones, says a lot more about you than about them. Clinging on to hurt, fury, and unfulfilled hopes will give you a pessimistic outlook on your partner's actions; this is not only unfair to them but also untrue. However, you cannot disregard reality. It is certainly possible that one's reservations may be true, but you need to focus way more on the gleeful sentiments than on the upsetting ones to maintain a happy relationship. If it's you adding the pessimism in your relationship on most occasions, maybe you're the real reason problems occur so often.

When time and again, you associate murk with your partner, be accountable. Reflect upon your contribution to all the hurdles before you go on to associate them wholly with your partner. Attempt to look towards what your partner excels in, and value those before you let yourself bask in their actions that upset you. When you make your partner's efforts prominent to yourself, it will also add tremendous amounts of happiness in your relationship besides allowing you to unleash your best qualities to them.

Am I Thoughtful Of The Ways My Partner Wants My Love For Them To Be Expressed?

Ideally, you should love your partner the same way you love yourself. But, what would you do if your partner asks for more? Maybe your partner looks for something like a romantic escape to a beachside, requiring a little more effort than you're willing to make? Or maybe a cliché dinner date? Won't it be a good idea to go the extra mile to make them feel valued? When people let themselves believe their partner longs for the same things they look for, it is most likely that they'll let their partner down in making them feel valued and loved.

Being humans, we often take shortcuts to express our sentiments because it's simpler that way. It's easy to make little gestures to make your partner feel loved but, actions such as listening, reflecting, and making efforts to go the extra mile require much more work. In the long run, relationships require compromises and growth. One needs to learn to reflect and be susceptible to change. Allow love to push you beyond your lines, and for them, be open to doing something that has more value to your partner than it does to you.

Self-Reflection: The Practice

Look For The Right Questions

Come up with a set of questions to routinely ask yourself as a means of self-evaluation. Some examples could be keeping track of stuff that makes you over overthink and whether they were worth the time. Question the reasons these thoughts make their way back to you and see what actions you're making to avoid them from occurring?

Fix A Time

Fixing a particular time to self-reflect will ensure you keep up with the practice, starting with a number as small as 10 minutes per day could be beneficial. With time, as you become skillful in this practice and eventually find yourself reflecting for lengthier times. The time itself doesn't suffice and requires you to commit to your practice, and when you do that, you'll be working your way to being a better partner.

Meditate

To some, it may sound uncomforting at first, but as you sit in peace and let your mind free to explore your thoughts, you'll begin to spot patterns; take note of these.

Keep A Journal

Jotting your thoughts down can prove very effective, and so, keep a journal for your thoughts that allow you to vent out your emotions on paper. This will also help in spotting trends in thoughts and actions.

Try A Writing Exercise

If you find your head flooding with thoughts, keep a timer of 5-10 minutes and jot everything down that you can think of. Does your mind feel jumbled with thoughts and decisions? Once you have them organized, search for patterns, and see if they are important enough to be on your paper.

An example could be where you feel your partner may be being disloyal to you. Once you write it down, see if maybe you're unnecessarily insecure. Consequently, catch the real problem and then work to tackle it.

Seek Nature

Strolling around, surrounded by nature, can help better your mood. With a better mood and a clearer mind, you're likely to stop overthinking on insignificant details. With a peaceful mind, you'll find a much clearer perspective to look at things with.

Talk To Yourself

Talking out loud can surprisingly lead to many realizations. When you converse with yourself, you let your thoughts out, and this eventually allows for self-reflection.

Do Breathing Exercises

The aim is to achieve a state of calmness, so, be it complex or simple breathing exercises; they'll all soothe you and allow you to think clearer.

Try Reading

Turning to read doesn't mean restricting yourself to self-improvement books only. Reading fiction novels, too, can be a great means of self-reflections as it brings a sort of meditation.

Assess An Event

First, select an event that bothered you. Second, take out time to assess the events that happened and question: Why do you feel a particular way about this incident? What was your contribution to this event? How could you possibly better react to it if it reoccurs?

Question What You Are Thankful For

When you finally get through a super busy and stressful day successfully, try sitting down and think about all the things you have to be thankful for. Make it a practice to count at least three things you are thankful for in your relationship.

For instance, all the support you get from your partner can be something to express gratitude for. How they constantly phone you to make sure you have eaten or how they respect and love your parents are some other examples.

Try Yoga

Yoga classes offer a soothing environment that can offer multiple benefits, such as flexibility and improved breathing.

During yoga, you'll notice that the soothing aspect of it triggers thoughts through meditations. This makes an ideal time to allow you to self-reflect.

Notice Trends In Your Emotions

Make use of a diary or an app so you could note your feelings every day. This will allow you to spot trends in your moods. The results may help you realize why you react a particular way; this, in turn, can bring peace of mind by giving you a clearer picture of your triggers.

Do A Self-Check Up

The easiest way to attempt this is to sit down, calm yourself, and analyze different domains of your life; career, academics, hobbies, family, health, financial independence raise questions such as:

- Are you facing any trouble with promotion at work?

- Are you not getting enough time to enjoy something

you love?

- Are you having any trouble with your parents or siblings?

- Are you satisfied with your contribution to each? If not, what could you improve?

Sometimes, you are not happy with a specific area of your life. As the frustration grows, you start projecting your worries onto your relationship in the form of overthinking. Reflecting on other areas of life can help overcome this problem.

Set Goals

Self-reflecting, in itself, isn't enough if done without determination. Hence, set goals and develop a constant frequency of reflecting. This will greatly boost growth. In other words, try asking yourself at what state you want to see yourself mentally and physically in the next six months, two years, or six years?

For example, you can set the following goals:

- You want to be in a stable relationship with your partner in the coming year

- You want to learn how to trust your partner even when things are not going the way you want to

- When you have a clear idea of these goals, turning them into reality is only a matter of commitment.

Try Counseling

A counselor provides a professional setting for you to disclose your thoughts. Your counselor will allow you to understand yourself way better and get self-reflection going much more effectively. Counseling will make you question your actions frequently, express your thoughts on papers, keep an eye on progress, and even offer multiple ways to make use of self-reflection.

Overthinking Versus Happiness

Have you still not found the perfect way to stop your habit of overthinking and destroying your long-distance relationship? Fret not, for there are additional ways to make sure you get there.

Meditation

Meditation is the best practice to clear your mind out of any clutter and damaging thoughts and start afresh.[25] There are several reasons why you should try meditation to give up on the habit of overthinking.

Meditation Sets Your Perspective Right

Overthinking in any relationship can plague your mind with unimportant ideas and thoughts. It can stress you out with suspicions, doubts, regrets, allusions, and distorted reality. None of these characteristics can help you live a peaceful and happy life. With meditation, you can clear your mind of all these thoughts by gaining a perspective. This practice will make you aware of the fact that a larger picture exists. You eventually realize that haunting thoughts are always parochial and restrictive. When you are finally ready to open up and explore more, you will be capable of joining the dots for larger pursuits in your relationship and life.

Meditation Helps You Overcome Negative Thoughts

Most of the time, you are always finding someone to fix the blame for the chaos in your life. For example, if you are having suspicious thoughts about your relationship, you tend to blame it on your partner for being so mistrustful. After all, it is easier to handle situations when you can point the finger at someone else instead of you. Meditation helps you overcome these traits like finger-pointing and fault-finding. It will help you get rid of overthinking and developing negative thoughts and promote the search for higher truths.

Guided Meditation

Now that you are well-aware of the benefits of meditation, it is time to learn how to perform the first type of meditation: the guided meditation.

First, you must settle down and take three long, deep breaths. With every breath, you let go, keep relaxing your body a bit more.

Once you realize that your body has come to a stop and is fully relaxed, it is the point when you start focusing on your mind. This is where the tricky part begins.

Next, you have to keep talking to yourself. Try saying things like, "I am aware that we have countless things to think about at the moment. I understand that I am anxious and insecure. I understand that I have to do something to save the future of our relationship. But right now, I just need to take out a minute to relax."

Constantly remind your mind that it is completely okay to let go of things that you cannot control. You cannot control who your partner sees or works with. You cannot control where he lives. So, let go of these thoughts and constantly remind yourself that "I am relaxed" and "I am at peace."

With this activity, you are training your brain to be at peace when you enter the state of meditation. A few sessions later, your brain will automatically know to relax whenever it hears the word 'meditation.'

Keep practicing this session as frequently as you like to release the stressful thoughts and be at peace. By the end of every session, your brain will be fresh, and you will be ready to rejoice in your relationship with a positive mindset.

Mindfulness Meditation

Following are some easy steps to practice mindful

meditation for overthinking:

1. Sit upright in a comfortable chair and put your feet flat on the floor.

2. Now pay attention to your breath. Avoid changing the way you are breathing. Simply focus on how your body is constantly inhaling and exhaling air.

3. You may feel the need to shift your focus to some other activity. Resist this urge as strongly as you can and maintain your focus.

4. Anxious thoughts will start flowing through your mind. You may acknowledge them, but remember to bring your attention back to your breathing.

5. Keep continuing this quiet observation for the next ten minutes.

6. Now open your eyes and observe how you feel.

The key to learning mindful practice is the acceptance of the world around you while maintaining curiosity. This meditative practice will soon spread to other areas of your life, such as your relationship. Then, you will learn how to observe the situation more deeply and calmly instead of reacting instantaneously. Your partner and relationship will thank you.

Exercise

Do you ever feel like you are unable to shut down your brain? Do the racing thoughts in your brain keep you awake all night, prevent you from falling asleep, and even if you do, they hit you as soon as you wake up? One simple way to calm down your overthinking brain is movement or exercise.

When you allow too many tensions and stressors to get on your brain, you train your brain to grow new neural pathways and accommodate them permanently. Then, your body keeps releasing relevant hormones and neurotransmitters to perpetuate these thoughts all the time. This perpetuation keeps on going to the extent that overthinking becomes your habit.

Luckily, exercise can help tame this overflow of thoughts. But how?

Physical activity or exercise can help utilize and burn any extra-adrenal or thyroid hormones that otherwise keep fueling your racing thoughts. The movement will also train your body to use up all the extra stress hormones in exercise. As a result, you feel a lot calmer and decrease your racing thoughts since you are re-training your neurology to focus on exercise. Additionally, performing regular workouts will increase the production of endorphins, the neurochemicals that generate feelings of happiness, and make you more efficient in everyday tasks. With exercise, you will be able to rest and sleep better and make better decisions. As a result, you can deal with your relationship issues more calmly and with more clarity.

Regular aerobic exercise is the best approach to clear your head of extra thoughts. This exercise will bring remarkable changes in your body, metabolism, spirits, and heart. This type of exercise has a unique ability to relax and exhilarate and to provide calm and stimulation. It can also tackle depression and manage the effective dissipation of stress. The best time to exercise is in the early hours of the morning or late afternoons, preferably before 7 pm. These are the times when they are tackling the highest level of stress.

Journaling

Another great way to get rid of the overthinking habit is journaling. The effects of journaling can be paramount in reducing overthinking and learning a lot about your psyche.[26] There are two types of journaling that you can benefit from.

Emotions/Feelings Journal

Emotions journal can help you release your feelings and emotions that you cannot let out to anyone, even your partner. To use this journal effectively, grab a pen, and follow the tips below.

Write Your Worries

Start your habit of journaling for five minutes to fifteen minutes per day. Write down everything that comes to your mind or bother you for long. Keep going like this until you feel like you have written down everything that you wish to, making sure you have not started ruminating, of course. You may use an actual journal, a simple notepad, or even your computer. It all depends on you.

Detail The Moment

Describe all the events that you think are creating hurdles for you. For example, your partner has been missing your video calls for a few days. Or maybe they do not text you as often as they did before. Sometimes, the problem is not what's happening in your life currently, but what could happen in the future. For instance, you might be worried that your partner does not want to turn this long-distance relationship into something permanent. Write down whatever's happening with you and note down that what's bothering you is a possibility, not a confirmed fact. This realization may bring relief.

List Your Fears

Make a list of all your fears and concerns following a chronological order. Begin with one stressor that you are currently facing. Then, write down what you think will happen next. Then, write down what you think will follow next. Don't forget to mention how you think it can affect you. Once you have all your fears and thoughts in order, you can try searching for different ways to relieve this stress.

Re-Read What You Just Wrote

Once you have finished writing all your thoughts, concerns, and fears in your journal, go through them when you are in a calm state of mind. Question yourself if these fears are valid? Is there a possibility that things are different? That you are not viewing the situation correctly.

Challenge Your Thoughts

As you are writing down your concerns and the things that are likely to happen, be critical. Try creating a self-argument. Write down every point that questions the reality and extent of your concern?

For example, if you think your partner is cheating on you, ask yourself:

- Why do you think so?

- How do you know this?

- Are you sure about this?

- If it happens, is there a possibility that it is less of a negative experience that you think it would be?

- Could you have done anything to avoid this?

Challenging your fears directly can reduce anxiety. It helps you visualize things that have little to no possibility of happening.

Gratitude Journal

If someone asks you what you are grateful for in your relationship, will you have an immediate answer? Will you be able to recall a moment with your partner that made you smile or brought joy? This simple habit of thinking about things you are grateful for can make your relationship and life a lot happier.

To do this, you can write a gratitude journal using the following tips.

Choose A Journal

The initial step to start working on a gratitude journal is to select a suitable journal. For this purpose, there are a few things that you can keep in mind. Do you prefer writing manually on a piece of paper, or do you prefer the digital mode? Would you like to carry your journal with you, or will you keep it in one place? Do you prefer lined or unlined pages? Consider all these factors and get the journal according to your preferences.

Set Aside Time For Writing

Finding time to write in your gratitude journal can be hard because it seems like a useless job among countless other chores on your list. However, once you form a routine, you will realize its benefits. To make sure you write in your gratitude journal daily, try attaching it to an existing habit. For example, you may write in it before going to bed or having your morning coffee.

Start With Gratitude Journal Prompts

If you are new to journaling, you may look at a blank page and wonder what to do with it. Some ideas to get you going include:

- Writing about the top three qualities in your partner that you are grateful for

- Writing about your favorite vacation spent with your partner and how happy it made you

Find What Works For You

One of the best things about gratitude journaling is that it does not have any rules. It is for you only, and you can choose to write it in any way you like. For example, if you are a visual person, you can try pasting photos of you and your partner on every page. Like doodling? How about you decorate all corners of your page using this art? This way, your journal will feel more personal to you, and you will want to open it every day.

Conclusion

Thank you for making it to the end of this book. Let's hope that this book was informative, and successfully provided you with all the tools, concepts, and ideas you need to make your relationship free of all dangers of overthinking. Let's also hope that with this book in your mind, you can visualize how overthinking is the reason behind the wreckage of your relationship.

Now, the next step for you to do is to reaffirm every single day that you are on a journey to become a better person. Keep reviewing how far you have come and been proud of it. Just like with anything, the key to your success depends on two things: determination and consistency. Before you can implement all the tips and tricks mentioned in this book, here is an additional tip for you. Always believe in yourself as well as your ability to make the changes necessary to save your relationship from overthinking. Then, move ahead to accomplish your goal. Once you successfully remove all the clutter from your find, you can use overthinking as a focused achievement.

Remember that overthinking is a poison, a poison that is slowly surrounding your relationship and making it weak from the very core. It is a venom that can take the life out of your relationship and hit the very thing that keeps your relationship happy and steady: trust. So, use this book as an anecdote to this poison and use it to the best of your abilities.

Good luck!

References

[1]   Bystritsky A, Liberman RP, Hwang S, Wallace CJ, Vapnik T, Maindment K, Saxena S. Social functioning and quality of life comparisons between obsessive-compulsive and schizophrenic disorders. Depression and Anxiety. 2001;14(4):214-8.

[2]   Munir S, Gondal AZ, Takov V. Generalized Anxiety Disorder (GAD). InStatPearls [Internet] 2019 Sep 15. StatPearls Publishing.

[3]   Roohafza H, Bidaki EZ, Hasanzadeh-Keshteli A, Daghaghzade H, Afshar H, Adibi P. Anxiety, depression and distress among irritable bowel syndrome and their subtypes: an epidemiological population based study. Advanced biomedical research. 2016;5.

[4]   Nguyen DT, Wright EP, Dedding C, Pham TT, Bunders J. Low self-esteem and its association with anxiety, depression, and suicidal ideation in Vietnamese secondary school students: a cross-sectional study. Frontiers in psychiatry. 2019 Sep 27;10:698.

[5]   Sansone RA, Sansone LA. Rumination: relationships with physical health. Innovations in clinical neuroscience. 2012 Feb 1;9(2):29.

[6]   Kuster F, Orth U, Meier LL. Rumination mediates the prospective effect of low self-esteem on depression: A five-wave longitudinal study. Personality and Social Psychology Bulletin. 2012 Jun;38(6):747-59.

[7]   Nolen-Hoeksema S, Wisco BE, Lyubomirsky S. Rethinking rumination. Perspectives on psychological science. 2008

Sep;3(5):400-24.

[8]   Hughes ME, Alloy LB, Cogswell A. Repetitive thought in psychopathology: The relation of rumination and worry to depression and anxiety symptoms. Journal of Cognitive Psychotherapy. 2008 Aug 1;22(3):271-88.

[9]   Kaiser BN, Haroz EE, Kohrt BA, Bolton PA, Bass JK, Hinton DE. "Thinking too much": A systematic review of a common idiom of distress. Social Science & Medicine. 2015 Dec 1;147:170-83.

[10]   Mroczkowski MM, Goes FS, Riddle MA, Grados MA, Bienvenu OJ, Greenberg BD, Fyer AJ, McCracken JT, Rauch SL, Murphy DL, Knowles JA. Dependent personality, separation anxiety disorder and other anxiety disorders in OCD. Personality and mental health. 2016 Feb;10(1):22-8.

[11]   Beckers T, Craske MG. Avoidance and decision making in anxiety: An introduction to the special issue. Behaviour research and therapy. 2017 Sep;96:1.

[12]   Coid J, Yang M, Bebbington P, Moran P, Brugha T, Jenkins R, Farrell M, Singleton N, Ullrich S. Borderline personality disorder: health service use and social functioning among a national household population. Psychological medicine. 2009 Oct;39(10):1721-31.

[13]   McLeod JD. Anxiety disorders and marital quality. Journal of Abnormal Psychology. 1994 Nov;103(4):767.

[14]   Avotri JY, Walters V. 'We Women Worry a Lot About Our Husbands': Ghanaian women talking about their health and their relationships with men. Journal of Gender Studies. 2001 Jul 1;10(2):197-211.

[15] Laborde ND, vanDommelen-Gonzalez E, Minnis AM. Trust–that's a big one: intimate partnership values among urban Latino youth. Culture, health & sexuality. 2014 Oct 21;16(9):1009-22.

[16] Dambrun M. Self-centeredness and selflessness: happiness correlates and mediating psychological processes. PeerJ. 2017 May 11;5:e3306.

[17] Rood L, Roelofs J, Bögels SM, Alloy LB. Dimensions of negative thinking and the relations with symptoms of depression and anxiety in children and adolescents. Cognitive therapy and research. 2010 Aug 1;34(4):333-42.

[18] Balon R. The importance of paying attention to relationships. Ann Clin Psychiatry. 2018 May 1;30:81-2.

[19] Krapf S. Moving in or breaking up? The role of distance in the development of romantic relationships. European Journal of Population. 2018 Aug 1;34(3):313-36.

[20] Lestari SB, Purbaningrum D, Naryoso A. The Management of Interpersonal Communication in A Long Distance Relationship Amongst college Students in The Context of Romantical Relationship (Studies on Diponegoro University Students who Undergo Long Distance Relationship with Their Partner). Interaksi Online. 2015 Dec 29;13(1).

[21] Lavner JA, Karney BR, Bradbury TN. Does couples' communication predict marital satisfaction, or does marital satisfaction predict communication?. Journal of Marriage and Family. 2016 Jun;78(3):680-94.

[22] Duval, S. and Wicklund, R.A., 1972. A theory of objective self awareness.

[23] Carlson EN, Vazire S, Furr RM. Meta-insight: Do people really know how others see them?. Journal of personality and social psychology. 2011 Oct;101(4):831.

[24] Rochat P. Five levels of self-awareness as they unfold early in life. Consciousness and cognition. 2003 Dec 1;12(4):717-31.

[25] Miller JJ, Fletcher K, Kabat-Zinn J. Three-year follow-up and clinical implications of a mindfulness meditation-based stress reduction intervention in the treatment of anxiety disorders. General hospital psychiatry. 1995 May 1;17(3):192-200.

[26] Smyth JM, Johnson JA, Auer BJ, Lehman E, Talamo G, Sciamanna CN. Online Positive Affect Journaling in the Improvement of Mental Distress and Well-Being in General Medical Patients With Elevated Anxiety Symptoms: A Preliminary Randomized Controlled Trial. JMIR mental health. 2018;5(4):e11290.

Disclaimer

The information contained in this book and its components, is meant to serve as a comprehensive collection of strategies that the author of this book has done research about. Summaries, strategies, tips and tricks are only recommendations by the author, and reading this book will not guarantee that one's results will exactly mirror the author's results.

The author of this book has made all reasonable efforts to provide current and accurate information for the readers of this book. The author and its associates will not be held liable for any unintentional errors or omissions that may be found.

The material in the book may include information by third-parties. Third-party materials comprise of opinions expressed by their owners. As such, the author of this book does not assume responsibility or liability for any third-party material or opinions.

The publication of third-party material does not constitute the author's guarantee of any information, products, services, or opinions contained within third-party material. Use of third-party material does not guarantee that your results will mirror our results. Publication of such third-party material is simply a recommendation and expression of the author's own opinion of that material.

Whether because of the progression of the Internet, or the unforeseen changes in company policy and editorial submission guidelines, what is stated as fact at the time of this writing may become outdated or inapplicable later.

written expressed and signed permission from the author.